UNCOMMON COMPETITOR

One-Day Contracts

A 30-day plan for individuals, teams, and companies who want to separate themselves from the competition.

SCOTT SAVOR

ISBN-13: 978-0-692-13166-4

DEDICATION

This book is dedicated to all the people who love to learn.

ACKNOWLEDGMENTS

To all the people who have crossed my path in life. I have learned
so much. Your exceptional love and support couldn't have
been any better. Everything I have done has been with
your help, and I will forever be grateful.

To Erika, my incredible wife, for her unconditional love and
sacrifice that made it possible for me to complete this work.

A special thanks to Anne Balke for her amazing
writing, editing and formatting skills. Her
support and vision were invaluable.

PREFACE

Sometimes you don't know what you've been missing until it arrives. Maybe for you, it has arrived right now. Today I challenge you to become an Uncommon Competitor; a highly disciplined and hyper-focused person in the pursuit of your purpose. From this point on, being common (blending in and living like everyone else) is no longer an option. It's time for you to separate yourself from the competition.

The most difficult work has already been done for you. I've been fortunate to have invested over 15,000 hours in education and training. The most effective competitors have been studied and their strategies simplified into 30, one-day contracts just for you. I'm confident that by living uncommonly myself I'll be able to teach you successfully. I look forward to helping you create a lifestyle that is full of competitive advantages that excite you so that you never have to worry about your competition again.

You'll earn the valuable attention of others if you execute the responsibilities in this book with clarity (clear understanding), creativity (unique way) and conviction (passionate confidence). Your influence will then increase by teaching what you have learned and living out your teaching. Take this process very seriously because you may only have one chance to impact a person's life. In addition to increasing your influence, your attitude, effort, and focus will be elevated to elite levels. Your improved skills will then create uncommon conversations that will attract inspired, like-minded individuals into your life. Be ready.

It's now time for you to compete uncommonly. Your goal for the next 30 days is to commit to the execution of all 30 contracts in this book. Get excited! Every contract has been created for any competitor, regardless of their skill level or situation. Even better, all of your future responsibilities are 100% controllable and only require minutes each day to complete. You have no excuses.

TABLE OF CONTENTS

INTRODUCTION

WHAT IS AN UNCOMMON COMPETITOR?

Most people struggle to separate themselves from the competition. In this day and age, it is essential to stand out from the crowd, that's a given. But sadly, instead of finding their own identity and uniqueness, many people compare themselves to others, and in turn, they try to replicate what their "competition" is doing.

Yes, there is power in modeling the habits of successful people, teams, and companies. However, the downside of this strategy is that if it is not mixed with behaviors and a vision that are in line with your own personal (team or company) core values, the end result is a bunch of "look-alikes."

Albert Einstein once said, "The definition of insanity is doing the same thing over and over and expecting different results." I couldn't agree more, and this includes the belief that by doing exactly what everyone else is doing, that you will have a competitive advantage. If you want to be different, you have to do something different – both in terms of your own actions and in terms of what others are doing.

I believe it's time for people to stop being common and start striving to be uncommon. What do I mean by this? Let's start by looking at two definitions:

- **Common** - occurring, found, or done often; prevalent.

- **Uncommon** - out of the ordinary; not ordinarily encountered, different, unusual.

In order to be an Uncommon Competitor, one who is not simply doing what is common, what is prevalent, and what everyone else is doing, it takes discipline and hyper-focus on the things which are in line with your sense of purpose. You need to wake up every day, excited about what you are doing, and what lies ahead of you.

Sadly, most people go through life, just getting by, struggling to

3

find purpose, or accepting life as it is, with no vision for something better. But you are reading this book, so I know that's not you!

Unlike most people, who never take the time to crystallize their beliefs and find their purpose, you are ready to take action. The trick is to crystallize your beliefs and core values, so that your vision is so strong that you won't be willing to compromise, no matter what the circumstances. Once identified, these will help you align and be attracted to other like-minded people in your industry.

Finding your core values, what really matters to you, is a personal journey (and the same is true for teams and companies, but in this case, it would be done as a group). But vision without action is just a dream. In order to accomplish your goals, it will take discipline, focus and positive daily habits. That's what this book is all about.

Whether you're an individual looking to raise your game to the next level, a team striving for the next championship, a company ready to break away from the competition, or someone who simply wants more out of life, then this book is for you! The daily activities in this book will help you create a lifestyle that contains the competitive advantages you need so that you never have to worry about your competition again.

I promise you, that while all of the actions you will take during the next 30 days are easy to do, they may not be "easy." Each responsibility is designed so that it is achievable, but some of them may require you to take a close look at your current habits, beliefs, and behaviors – ones that may actually be holding you back in the pursuit of your purpose.

Each of the daily focuses in this book comes from studying effective competitors and is based upon proven strategies. Now it's up to you to implement and personalize them in order to develop your own unique values and vision for your life. Remember, to be uncommon, you have to do the uncommon.

WHAT MAKES THIS BOOK DIFFERENT?

If you are looking for a book filled with theories, long explanations, and lots of examples, this is not it. Don't get me wrong, there is absolutely nothing wrong with books like that. I am a firm believer in reading for both knowledge and pleasure, having read and listened to over 10,000 books in my lifetime, on subjects such as motivation, philosophy, wealth, performance, psychology, leadership and business. But what I have learned in my experience as a personal development coach, is that people often get stuck in the "learning phase," looking for the perfect answers or strategies, waiting to take action until everything is lined up just the right way.

This is book is about doing – taking steps to create changes and develop positive habits, even when we don't know the answers. There is a Latin proverb – Fortune favors the bold. Sometimes translated as fortune favors the strong, but either way, this expression truly applies to Uncommon Competitors. They take action, unafraid of making mistakes, knowing full well that if things don't go according to plan, the end result is a learning experience and an opportunity for improvement.

With the exception of these first few introductory pages, the remainder of this book contains time-tested actions, one per day, that when implemented with conviction and a commitment to your own growth, are guaranteed to put you on a path towards standing out from the crowd as an Uncommon Competitor.

Another thing that makes this book different from many others is that instead of focusing on the same goal, over and over, each contract has a different focus. For example, instead of practicing gratitude for 30 days straight, there is only one daily contract for this focus. Why? There are two reasons for this:

1. This book is about forming the habit of taking action and starting each day with a specific focus.

2. To provide variety, prevent boredom and to start each day with a new, fresh focus for the day.

Does this mean you should not have a mindset of gratefulness, each and every day? Of course not. But on the day that you choose to complete the focus of gratitude, your goal is to be more mindful of it, and complete the responsibilities included in the contract. The same is true with the other 29 focuses. By switching things up daily, my hope for you is to start each day with a sense of excitement, eager for what the day will bring.

Each daily focus is presented in the form of a contract – one you are going to be making with yourself, the Uncommon Competitor. Yes, I acknowledge that for many people, contracts can be a bit intimidating, even scary. When presented with a legal contract, it signifies a commitment, one that you are signing your name to. We do not enter into legal contracts lightly, because we know that there are repercussions for breaking them.

In life, we are used to making contracts with, or making promises to, others. Yet, how often do we make promises to ourselves, or commit to doing something, only to not fulfill what we said we were going to do? For many people, the person that gets let down the most is ourselves. The use of a contract format was intentional because taking actions for ourselves is serious business. In order to become an Uncommon Competitor, you must be able to make and keep, commitments that you make to yourself.

Just like a traditional contract is signed by a witness, so will your daily contracts. The responsibilities of the witness are two-fold: to hold yourself accountable, but more importantly, to be someone who can you can share what you learned and score your teaching ability for each day. When we take the opportunity to speak out loud and teach another, it reinforces the learning process. It also gives you the opportunity for both open feedback, as well as spreading new information to another, who may potentially take this information and pass it along.

Before we move on to how to choose a witness, let's take a moment to talk about the teaching process, and how it should be scored by your witness. When you approach someone to be your witness who is not doing the contracts within this book, it is important to tell them a bit about what you're doing. Depending upon your relationship with the person, you may want to go into more detail, but minimally you want to let them know that you are working on developing new positive habits and need their help. Something as simple as – *"Hey, do you have a few minutes now, or later today? I am learning something new and need to see if I know it well enough to teach it to someone?"* – will do the trick.

When it's time to sit down and share what you have learned, it is important to tell your witness that you want honest feedback. Share that you are serious about this process, and want them to score you honestly, so that you can learn and make improvements along the journey. You will be asking them to give you a score for each of these areas:

- **Clarity:** Were you able to convey your knowledge of the focus of the day in a manner that was clearly understood? Were you able to answer any questions that the witness had about the focus and what it means?

- **Creativity:** Did you teach the information in a way that was unique? Did you put the focus of the day in your own words, making it personal to you? Or did you simply repeat back what was on the contract?

- **Conviction:** Did you teach with passion and confidence? Were you excited about what you had learned? Did you enthusiastically talk about the impact completing the responsibilities had on your day, and/or how you could apply the new information to your life?

Scoring for each of these criteria will be on a scale of 1 to 3, with the lower indicating average performance and the upper indicating superior performance. At the end of the month, you will tally your total score to get an overall "Competitor Level" rating. You will also be able to use individual daily scores to evaluate things such as which habits excited you more than others, which ones you struggled with and areas where you need improvement. An added benefit of this process is that it helps to improve communication and public speaking skills. If this is something you struggle with right now, some of your scores may be lower at the start of the month, but as you complete more of the teaching responsibilities, you should see your numbers go up!

If your scores are lower than you had hoped for, especially at the start, don't be discouraged. The fact that you are implementing these new habits and completing daily contracts already puts you ahead of the masses on the road to becoming Uncommon. Don't give up on your commitment to yourself and keep going for the full 30 days. **Commitment is not a guarantee of anything, but a requirement of everything!**

When it comes to choosing a witness, there are many ways to go about it. The most important consideration in this process is to select someone who is competitive and who will challenge you. It should not be easy for you to earn a "superior" score when they evaluate your teaching ability.

Witnesses can be family, friends, co-workers, or even complete strangers (for those of you bold enough to step out of your comfort zone). Some of the responsibilities are ones that require choosing a specific person, and in that case, that person would be the witness. Unless you are working within a team or company who has chosen an approach with accountability partners, the best results will come from switching things up and not always using the same witness every day.

There is no right or wrong way to go through the contracts in this book, all that matters is that you do a different one each day. Some of you may choose to work through them in order. Some may pick ones that are easier first, while others may choose to start with the more difficult ones. Others may decide to mix it up.

Whatever you decide works best for you, resist the urge to repeat a focus for more than one day. Also, if you found a particular focus to be more difficult, perhaps not being able to complete it, wipe the slate clean and don't dwell on it when you start your next day. Praise yourself and give yourself a pat on the back for the fact that you took action. At the end of the 30 days, take the time to look back at all you have accomplished.

Before you get started with your first contract, it is important to establish a reward for the end of the 30 days. Remember, what gets done gets rewarded, and what gets rewarded gets done. This may sound like a basic principle, one we learned as children from our parents, teachers, and coaches. Think about how great it felt to get a gold star on school work, received a trophy for an achievement or when you were taken out for ice cream for a special accomplishment.

Yet as adults, somehow, we forget how powerful rewards can be. They make us feel good about what we are doing, and in turn, we want to do more of it. There are two ways to use this book – individually, or as part of a group (team or company) – and the reward used may depend upon the circumstances.

- **Individuals -** If you are using this book as a tool for your own personal development, it's up to you to choose a reward that is significant, and one worth working for. You may choose one powerful reward for successfully completing all 30, and a different one for let's say accomplishing at least 20.

  Make sure to follow through with your reward! You may even want to put a picture of your reward on your refrigerator, bathroom mirror, or tucked inside this book as a daily reminder.

- **Groups (Teams or Companies) -** If you are part of a group that is working on this book together, there is even more power within these pages. When members of a group, working together, are exposed to things that they can do that will move the needle, I can say with 100% certainty that you will see positive changes and growth. This is about creating a culture, within a team or company, where everyone is on the same page, encouraging and supporting each other.

In terms of rewards, there is much to choose from, but keep in mind that praise and recognition are among the ones that hold the most power for people. Also, it is important that you do not structure this in a way that is a competition for who can out-do others or one department against another. While you may have different rewards for the people who achieve the highest number of contracts completed, it's even more valuable to celebrate the process on a day to day basis with specific verbal praise.

You may also want to be mindful of how you use monetary rewards. Believe it or not, research has shown that this type of reward, without the proper education, can actually have a de-motivating effect. If you do want to use a financial reward, educate the participants that although the amount may not be exactly what they desire, the goal is to increase gratitude and reward the process.

For the best results, ask the person (or team members) what reward they desire, for example:

- ♦ Money or a gift (tangible item),

- ♦ Group party or awards gathering (celebration of achievements),

- ♦ Self-directed responsibility (autonomy),

- ♦ Paid training opportunity (mastery), or

- ♦ Responsibility not linked to outcome or profit (purpose).

Regardless of which reward you ultimately use, don't skip the reward of recognition. You may want to create certificates of achievement or post a wall of fame that acknowledges the progress of the team. Get the team involved in the process and have fun with it!

In closing, to maximize this book, select only one contract of your choice and execute it by the end of that calendar day. Continue the process for the next 30 days, choosing a different contract each day. Be sure to review each contract in detail and prioritize the responsibilities.

Whether you are participating by yourself, with a team or a company, don't forget to build in that reward for completing contracts after 30 days.

Are you ready to get started on the path to becoming an Uncommon Competitor? Your time is now!

RECORDING YOUR PROGRESS

Use this chart to track your daily progress. Before the end of each day, record the completion date and the total score from the competitor teaching evaluation. After 30 days, use the scale at the end of the book to see how well you did.

Name of Contract	Date	Score
Earn It	1/7	
Total Recall		
Family Tree		
Ground Zero		
Positively Negative		
Pep Talk		
Zero Dark Thirty		
N.O.C. List - No Other Calls List		
Sundown Rule		
Non-Dominant Dominance		
ABC's of Gratitude		
A-Game - Awareness Game		
Limitless		
If You Only Knew		
Survival of the Wisest		
Worst-Case Scenario		
Got Your Back		
Get Your Mind Right		
Performance Playlist		
Proud Purchase		
Strength in Numbers		
Give Up to Go Up		
Cell Phone Roulette		
Refuel		
Built for the Grind		
Dedication Day		
Personal Thank You		
Change the World List		
Li'l Mo - Little Momentum		
F.O.T.D. - Failure Of The Day		
Total Scores	/30	/270

EARN IT

The more you get what you want, the harder it is to act when you don't get what you want.

EARN IT

I, _____*Alex Aria*_____, hereby enter into this
contract with myself, the Uncommon Competitor, and commit to
learning TODAY'S FOCUS and completing all of the outlined
RESPONSIBILITIES for the day.

_____*alex H*_____   __1__ / __7__ / 20__20__
Competitor (Signature)   Date

I. TODAY'S FOCUS

The more you get for free, the less you will be free.
Uncommon Competitors are always asking to earn things.
You must respectfully reject many things people give you for
free so that you can guard your appetite and appreciation!

II. RESPONSIBILITIES

(1) Ask one person today: "How can I earn ___*focus*___?"
Write down their reaction and the specific request that
they made. No matter what you chose to earn be sure it
wasn't easy.

(2) Select a witness and teach them what you learned. Have
them evaluate your teaching, give you a score and sign.

COMPETITOR TEACHING EVALUATION	
1 = Average 2 = Above Average 3 = Superior	
Clarity: Did they know the content and teach it clearly?	
Creativity: Did they teach in a unique way?	
Conviction: Did they teach with passion and confidence?	
Total Score	/9

IN WITNESS WHEREOF, I, _____,
confirm that the Uncommon Competitor has completed the
contract and I have honestly evaluated their teaching.

_____   ____ / ____ / 20____
Witness (Signature)   Date

NOTES – EARN IT

- Need to highlight ✓
  Key?

- Communicate effectively ✓

- next lon l ✓

- prep sheet ✓

18

NOTES – EARN IT

_____

_____

_____

_____

_____

_____

_____

_____

_____

_____

_____

_____

_____

_____

_____

_____

_____

_____

_____

_____

_____

_____

_____

Work so hard you no longer need introductions.

Anonymous

LEARN & LIVE – EARN IT

Now that you have completed today's contract and have had it
scored, take a moment before you go to bed and answer the
following questions:

What was I most proud of?

Execution after preparation
effort

What was I least proud of?

Avoiding conflict

What did I learn about myself?

Truly don't expect
they know

What will I do differently in the future?

Truly just don't
expect

TOTAL
RECALL

Discipline is
remembering what
you want.

TOTAL RECALL

I, _____*Alex H*_____, hereby enter into this
contract with myself, the Uncommon Competitor, and commit to
learning TODAY'S FOCUS and completing all of the outlined
RESPONSIBILITIES for the day.

_____*Alex H*_____   _____/____/20_20_ → *failed*
      Competitor (Signature)   Date

                                        1/13/2020

I. TODAY'S FOCUS

**It's not what you know but what you have forgotten that
matters.** Uncommon Competitors forget less and recall
what's most important because they have help. You must set
up your day with creative reminders that help you so that you
can stay hyper-focused!

II. RESPONSIBILITIES

(1) Create one reminder (write on your hand, make a list, put
an item in your pocket, etc.) to think, act or feel
something important today. It doesn't matter what the
reminder is, just as long as it stays close to you.

(2) Select a witness and teach them what you learned. Have
them evaluate your teaching, give you a score and sign.

COMPETITOR TEACHING EVALUATION	
1 = Average 2 = Above Average 3 = Superior	
Clarity: Did they know the content and teach it clearly?	
Creativity: Did they teach in a unique way?	
Conviction: Did they teach with passion and confidence?	
Total Score	/9

IN WITNESS WHEREOF, I, _____,
confirm that the Uncommon Competitor has completed the
contract and I have honestly evaluated their teaching.

_____   _____/____/20____
      Witness (Signature)   Date

23

- be the crazy
  they need

- overbelieve — lead
  others

NOTES – TOTAL RECALL

_____

_____

_____

_____

_____

_____

_____

_____

_____

_____

_____

_____

_____

_____

_____

_____

_____

_____

_____

_____

_____

_____

_____

When declaring your rights,
don't forget your responsibilities.

H. Jackson Brown Jr.

LEARN & LIVE – TOTAL RECALL

Now that you have completed today's contract and have had it scored, take a moment before you go to bed and answer the following questions:

What was I most proud of?

_____

_____

_____

_____

What was I least proud of?

_____

_____

_____

_____

What did I learn about myself?

_____

_____

_____

_____

What will I do differently in the future?

_____

_____

_____

_____

FAMILY
TREE

When everything goes wrong, the people who stand by you without flinching are your family.

FAMILY TREE

I, _____*Alex Hij*_____, hereby enter into this
contract with myself, the Uncommon Competitor, and commit to
learning TODAY'S FOCUS and completing all of the outlined
RESPONSIBILITIES for the day.

_____   ___ / ___ / 20_10_
Competitor (Signature)   Date

I. TODAY'S FOCUS

The goal is to help friends become family. Uncommon
Competitors share their family situation with others. You
must communicate personal challenges and celebrations so
that others can grow closer to you!

II. RESPONSIBILITIES

(1) Diagram your family tree for one person. Write down the
     names of your parents, spouse, siblings, children, etc.
     Share what influence each person has had on your life.

(2) Select a witness and teach them what you learned. Have
     them evaluate your teaching, give you a score and sign.

COMPETITOR TEACHING EVALUATION	
1 = Average 2 = Above Average 3 = Superior	
Clarity: Did they know the content and teach it clearly?	
Creativity: Did they teach in a unique way?	
Conviction: Did they teach with passion and confidence?	
Total Score	/9

IN WITNESS WHEREOF, I, _____,
confirm that the Uncommon Competitor has completed the
contract and I have honestly evaluated their teaching.

_____   ___ / ___ / 20___
Witness (Signature)   Date

29

NOTES – FAMILY TREE

NOTES – FAMILY TREE

_____

_____

_____

_____

_____

_____

_____

_____

_____

_____

_____

_____

_____

_____

_____

_____

_____

_____

_____

_____

Friends are the family we choose for ourselves.

Edna Buchanan

LEARN & LIVE – FAMILY TREE

Now that you have completed today's contract and have had it
scored, take a moment before you go to bed and answer the
following questions:

What was I most proud of?

_____

_____

_____

_____

What was I least proud of?

_____

_____

_____

_____

What did I learn about myself?

_____

_____

_____

_____

What will I do differently in the future?

_____

_____

_____

_____

GROUND
ZERO

When the mind is not present, we look and do not see; we hear and do not understand; we eat and do not know the taste of what we eat.

GROUND ZERO

I, _____, hereby enter into this contract with myself, the Uncommon Competitor, and commit to learning TODAY'S FOCUS and completing all of the outlined RESPONSIBILITIES for the day.

_____   ____ / ____ / 20____
Competitor (Signature)   Date

I. TODAY'S FOCUS

Surround yourself with people because of their presence, not presents. Uncommon Competitors stay grounded to the present moment. You must activate all your senses at the highest level so that you can increase your presence!

II. RESPONSIBILITIES

(1) One time today identify and write down: five things you see, four things you feel, three things you hear, two things you smell and one thing you taste.

(2) Select a witness and teach them what you learned. Have them evaluate your teaching, give you a score and sign.

COMPETITOR TEACHING EVALUATION	
1 = Average 2 = Above Average 3 = Superior	
Clarity: Did they know the content and teach it clearly?	
Creativity: Did they teach in a unique way?	
Conviction: Did they teach with passion and confidence?	
Total Score	/9

IN WITNESS WHEREOF, I, _____,
confirm that the Uncommon Competitor has completed the contract and I have honestly evaluated their teaching.

_____   ____ / ____ / 20____
Witness (Signature)   Date

NOTES – GROUND ZERO

NOTES – GROUND ZERO

_____

_____

_____

_____

_____

_____

_____

_____

_____

_____

_____

_____

_____

_____

_____

_____

_____

_____

_____

Wherever you are be all there.

Jim Elliot

LEARN & LIVE – GROUND ZERO

Now that you have completed today's contract and have had it scored, take a moment before you go to bed and answer the following questions:

What was I most proud of?

_____

_____

_____

_____

What was I least proud of?

_____

_____

_____

_____

What did I learn about myself?

_____

_____

_____

_____

What will I do differently in the future?

_____

_____

_____

_____

POSITIVELY
NEGATIVE

If you realized how powerful your thoughts were, you would never have a negative thought.

POSITIVELY NEGATIVE

I, _____Alex Hu_____, hereby enter into this
contract with myself, the Uncommon Competitor, and commit to
learning TODAY'S FOCUS and completing all of the outlined
RESPONSIBILITIES for the day.

_____   __1_/_16_/ 20_20_
Competitor (Signature)   Date

I. TODAY'S FOCUS

**Telling the truth and making someone cry is better than
telling a lie and making someone smile.** Uncommon
Competitors positively navigate negative conversations. You
must hear what you fear so that you are calm in any debate!

II. RESPONSIBILITIES

(1) Take turns sharing sensitive truths with one person (You
don't listen. I can't count on you. You're lazy…) Stay
confident, remain optimistic and have fun with it.

(2) Select a witness and teach them what you learned. Have
them evaluate your teaching, give you a score and sign.

COMPETITOR TEACHING EVALUATION	
1 = Average 2 = Above Average 3 = Superior	
Clarity: Did they know the content and teach it clearly?	
Creativity: Did they teach in a unique way?	
Conviction: Did they teach with passion and confidence?	
Total Score	/9

IN WITNESS WHEREOF, I, _____,
confirm that the Uncommon Competitor has completed the
contract and I have honestly evaluated their teaching.

_____   ____/____/ 20____
Witness (Signature)   Date

NOTES – POSITIVELY NEGATIVE

NOTES – POSITIVELY NEGATIVE

_____

_____

_____

_____

_____

_____

_____

_____

_____

_____

_____

_____

_____

_____

_____

_____

_____

_____

_____

_____

_____

_____

_____

_____

The test of a first-rate intelligence is the ability to hold two opposed ideas in mind at the same time and still retain the ability to function.

F. Scott Fitzgerald

LEARN & LIVE – POSITIVELY NEGATIVE

Now that you have completed today's contract and have had it scored, take a moment before you go to bed and answer the following questions:

What was I most proud of?

_____

_____

_____

_____

What was I least proud of?

_____

_____

_____

_____

What did I learn about myself?

_____

_____

_____

_____

What will I do differently in the future?

_____

_____

_____

_____

PEP TALK

Actions prove who someone is, words prove who they want to be.

PEP TALK

I, _____*Alex Hein*_____, hereby enter into this
contract with myself, the Uncommon Competitor, and commit to
learning TODAY'S FOCUS and completing all of the outlined
RESPONSIBILITIES for the day.

_____*Alex H.*_____   __1__ / __24__ / 20__20__
Competitor (Signature)   Date

I. <u>TODAY'S FOCUS</u>

**Speak to yourself like you are the most important person
in the world and everyone needs you.** Uncommon
Competitors give pep talks to boost their energy. You must
speak with inspiration so that others will listen to you!

II. <u>RESPONSIBILITIES</u>

(1) In front of others read out loud: "Invictus" by William
Ernest Henley, "It's Up to Me" by James J. Metcalfe or the
last prayer from the movie *The Book of Eli.*

(2) Select a witness and teach them what you learned. Have
them evaluate your teaching, give you a score and sign.

COMPETITOR TEACHING EVALUATION	
1 = Average 2 = Above Average 3 = Superior	
Clarity: Did they know the content and teach it clearly?	
Creativity: Did they teach in a unique way?	
Conviction: Did they teach with passion and confidence?	
Total Score	/9

IN WITNESS WHEREOF, I, _____,
confirm that the Uncommon Competitor has completed the
contract and I have honestly evaluated their teaching.

_____   ____ / ____ / 20____
Witness (Signature)   Date

47

NOTES – PEP TALK

NOTES – PEP TALK

_____

_____

_____

_____

_____

_____

_____

_____

_____

_____

_____

_____

_____

_____

_____

_____

_____

_____

_____

*Be careful with your words, once they are said,
they can only be forgiven, not forgotten.*

Carl Sandburg

LEARN & LIVE – PEP TALK

Now that you have completed today's contract and have had it scored, take a moment before you go to bed and answer the following questions:

What was I most proud of?

_____

_____

_____

_____

What was I least proud of?

_____

_____

_____

_____

What did I learn about myself?

_____

_____

_____

_____

What will I do differently in the future?

_____

_____

_____

_____

ZERO DARK
THIRTY

Attention is the
rarest and purest
form of generosity.

ZERO DARK THIRTY

I, _____, hereby enter into this contract with myself, the Uncommon Competitor, and commit to learning TODAY'S FOCUS and completing all of the outlined RESPONSIBILITIES for the day.

_____   ____ / ____ / 20____
Competitor (Signature)   Date

I. TODAY'S FOCUS

The most dangerous distractions are the ones you love but don't love you back. Uncommon Competitors don't hesitate to go completely dark from social media. You must decrease distractions so that you can narrow your focus!

II. RESPONSIBILITIES

(1) Turn off all social media notifications on your digital devices. Do not check any of your media for the entire day (unless required for work or safety).

(2) Select a witness and teach them what you learned. Have them evaluate your teaching, give you a score and sign.

COMPETITOR TEACHING EVALUATION	
1 = Average 2 = Above Average 3 = Superior	
Clarity: Did they know the content and teach it clearly?	
Creativity: Did they teach in a unique way?	
Conviction: Did they teach with passion and confidence?	
Total Score	/9

IN WITNESS WHEREOF, I, _____, confirm that the Uncommon Competitor has completed the contract and I have honestly evaluated their teaching.

_____   ____ / ____ / 20____
Witness (Signature)   Date

NOTES – ZERO DARK THIRTY

_____

_____

_____

_____

_____

_____

_____

_____

_____

_____

_____

_____

_____

_____

_____

_____

_____

_____

_____

_____

Do not fear to lose what needs to be lost.

Sue Monk Kidd

LEARN & LIVE – ZERO DARK THIRTY

Now that you have completed today's contract and have had it scored, take a moment before you go to bed and answer the following questions:

What was I most proud of?

_____

_____

_____

_____

What was I least proud of?

_____

_____

_____

_____

What did I learn about myself?

_____

_____

_____

_____

What will I do differently in the future?

_____

_____

_____

_____

N.O.C. LIST

Show me your
friends, and I'll show
you your future.

N.O.C. LIST

I, _____, hereby enter into this
contract with myself, the Uncommon Competitor, and commit to
learning TODAY'S FOCUS and completing all of the outlined
RESPONSIBILITIES for the day.

_____   ____ / ____ / 20____
Competitor (Signature)   Date

I. TODAY'S FOCUS

**Stay in contact with others who can change your life, not
just change your status.** Uncommon Competitors only
allow a "No Other Calls" contact list in their phone. You
must upgrade your contacts so that you can upgrade your life!

II. RESPONSIBILITIES

(1) Edit your phone contacts to only these: relatives (family),
resources (one who solves a problem) and refrigerator
rights (one you trust to take something without asking).

(2) Select a witness and teach them what you learned. Have
them evaluate your teaching, give you a score and sign.

COMPETITOR TEACHING EVALUATION	
1 = Average 2 = Above Average 3 = Superior	
Clarity: Did they know the content and teach it clearly?	
Creativity: Did they teach in a unique way?	
Conviction: Did they teach with passion and confidence?	
Total Score	/9

IN WITNESS WHEREOF, I, _____,
confirm that the Uncommon Competitor has completed the
contract and I have honestly evaluated their teaching.

_____   ____ / ____ / 20____
Witness (Signature)   Date

NOTES – N.O.C. LIST

NOTES – N.O.C. LIST

_____

_____

_____

_____

_____

_____

_____

_____

_____

_____

_____

_____

_____

_____

_____

_____

_____

_____

_____

_____

The fastest way to change yourself is to hang out with people who are already the way you want to be.

Reid Hoffman

LEARN & LIVE – N.O.C. LIST

Now that you have completed today's contract and have had it scored, take a moment before you go to bed and answer the following questions:

What was I most proud of?

_____

_____

_____

_____

What was I least proud of?

_____

_____

_____

_____

What did I learn about myself?

_____

_____

_____

_____

What will I do differently in the future?

_____

_____

_____

_____

SUNDOWN RULE

Don't text me and I'll understand, don't call me I'll understand, and if I forget you, you'll understand.

SUNDOWN RULE

I, _____, hereby enter into this
contract with myself, the Uncommon Competitor, and commit to
learning TODAY'S FOCUS and completing all of the outlined
RESPONSIBILITIES for the day.

_____   ____ / ____ / 20____
Competitor (Signature)   Date

I. TODAY'S FOCUS

Great communicators listen to what people don't say.
Uncommon Competitors reply to others before the sun goes
down. You must make simple, same day communication a
priority so that others know that they are important to you!

II. RESPONSIBILITIES

(1) Respond simply to as many unanswered messages as you
can. Say: "Thanks for the message. Is there anything else I
can do?" Your goal is to have zero "unread" or "new"
messages before the sun goes down.

(2) Select a witness and teach them what you learned. Have
them evaluate your teaching, give you a score and sign.

COMPETITOR TEACHING EVALUATION	
1 = Average 2 = Above Average 3 = Superior	
Clarity: Did they know the content and teach it clearly?	
Creativity: Did they teach in a unique way?	
Conviction: Did they teach with passion and confidence?	
Total Score	/9

IN WITNESS WHEREOF, I, _____,
confirm that the Uncommon Competitor has completed the
contract and I have honestly evaluated their teaching.

_____   ____ / ____ / 20____
Witness (Signature)   Date

NOTES – SUNDOWN RULE

NOTES – SUNDOWN RULE

_____

_____

_____

_____

_____

_____

_____

_____

_____

_____

_____

_____

_____

_____

_____

_____

_____

_____

_____

In teamwork, silence isn't golden, it's deadly.

Mark Sanborn

LEARN & LIVE – SUNDOWN RULE

Now that you have completed today's contract and have had it scored, take a moment before you go to bed and answer the following questions:

What was I most proud of?

_____

_____

_____

_____

What was I least proud of?

_____

_____

_____

_____

What did I learn about myself?

_____

_____

_____

_____

What will I do differently in the future?

_____

_____

_____

_____

NON-DOMINANT
DOMINANCE

Whatever makes you
uncomfortable is your
biggest opportunity
for growth.

NON-DOMINANT DOMINANCE

I, _____, hereby enter into this contract with myself, the Uncommon Competitor, and commit to learning TODAY'S FOCUS and completing all of the outlined RESPONSIBILITIES for the day.

_____   ____ / ____ / 20____
Competitor (Signature)   Date

I. TODAY'S FOCUS

Every time you choose comfort you reinforce fear.
Uncommon Competitors dominate non-optimal opportunities on purpose. You must consistently change how you do things so that you can be comfortable being uncomfortable!

II. RESPONSIBILITIES

(1) Perform activities with your non-dominate limbs (brush teeth, text, eat, drink, etc.). Compete with laser-like focus, no fear of failure and remember to enjoy the journey.

(2) Select a witness and teach them what you learned. Have them evaluate your teaching, give you a score and sign.

COMPETITOR TEACHING EVALUATION	
1 = Average 2 = Above Average 3 = Superior	
Clarity: Did they know the content and teach it clearly?	
Creativity: Did they teach in a unique way?	
Conviction: Did they teach with passion and confidence?	
Total Score	/9

IN WITNESS WHEREOF, I, _____, confirm that the Uncommon Competitor has completed the contract and I have honestly evaluated their teaching.

_____   ____ / ____ / 20____
Witness (Signature)   Date

NOTES – NON-DOMINANT DOMINANCE

NOTES – NON-DOMINANT DOMINANCE

_____

_____

_____

_____

_____

_____

_____

_____

_____

_____

_____

_____

_____

_____

_____

_____

_____

_____

_____

_____

_____

*You are free to choose, but you are not free
from the consequences of your choices.*

Zig Ziglar

LEARN & LIVE – NON-DOMINANT DOMINANCE

Now that you have completed today's contract and have had it scored, take a moment before you go to bed and answer the following questions:

What was I most proud of?

_____

_____

_____

_____

What was I least proud of?

_____

_____

_____

_____

What did I learn about myself?

_____

_____

_____

_____

What will I do differently in the future?

_____

_____

_____

_____

ABC'S OF GRATITUDE

Love what you have
before life teaches you
to love what you lost.

ABC'S OF GRATITUDE

I, _____, hereby enter into this contract with myself, the Uncommon Competitor, and commit to learning TODAY'S FOCUS and completing all of the outlined RESPONSIBILITIES for the day.

_____   ____ / ____ / 20____
Competitor (Signature)   Date

I. TODAY'S FOCUS

If you have nothing to be grateful for, check your pulse.
Uncommon Competitors can access countless forms of gratitude quickly. You must make the pleasure greater than the pressure so that you can reduce the stresses in your life!

II. RESPONSIBILITIES

(1) Quickly write down a word for each letter of the alphabet that you're grateful for (A-Adversity, B-Bravery, C-Challenges, etc.). Record the time it took to complete.

(2) Select a witness and teach them what you learned. Have them evaluate your teaching, give you a score and sign.

COMPETITOR TEACHING EVALUATION	
1 = Average 2 = Above Average 3 = Superior	
Clarity: Did they know the content and teach it clearly?	
Creativity: Did they teach in a unique way?	
Conviction: Did they teach with passion and confidence?	
Total Score	/9

IN WITNESS WHEREOF, I, _____, confirm that the Uncommon Competitor has completed the contract and I have honestly evaluated their teaching.

_____   ____ / ____ / 20____
Witness (Signature)   Date

NOTES – ABC'S OF GRATITUDE

NOTES – ABC'S OF GRATITUDE

_____

_____

_____

_____

_____

_____

_____

_____

_____

_____

_____

_____

_____

_____

_____

_____

_____

_____

_____

_____

*The real gift of gratitude is that the more grateful you are,
the more present you become.*

Robert Holden

LEARN & LIVE – ABC'S OF GRATITUDE

Now that you have completed today's contract and have had it scored, take a moment before you go to bed and answer the following questions:

What was I most proud of?

_____

_____

_____

_____

What was I least proud of?

_____

_____

_____

_____

What did I learn about myself?

_____

_____

_____

_____

What will I do differently in the future?

_____

_____

_____

_____

A-GAME

You don't mature
through age, you
mature through
awareness.

A-GAME

I, _____, hereby enter into this
contract with myself, the Uncommon Competitor, and commit to
learning TODAY'S FOCUS and completing all of the outlined
RESPONSIBILITIES for the day.

_____   ____ /____ / 20____
    Competitor (Signature)   Date

I. TODAY'S FOCUS

The greater your awareness, the greater your power.
Uncommon Competitors play the "Awareness Game" to
notice what others don't. You must observe the intricate
details of all environments so that you activate your abilities!

II. RESPONSIBILITIES

(1) Write down your answers to the following questions:
"Who was the most passionate person you noticed today?
Most positive? Most focused? Most grateful? Why?"

(2) Select a witness and teach them what you learned. Have
them evaluate your teaching, give you a score and sign.

COMPETITOR TEACHING EVALUATION	
1 = Average 2 = Above Average 3 = Superior	
Clarity: Did they know the content and teach it clearly?	
Creativity: Did they teach in a unique way?	
Conviction: Did they teach with passion and confidence?	
Total Score	**/9**

IN WITNESS WHEREOF, I, _____,
confirm that the Uncommon Competitor has completed the
contract and I have honestly evaluated their teaching.

_____   ____ /____ / 20____
    Witness (Signature)   Date

NOTES – A-GAME

_____

_____

_____

_____

_____

_____

_____

_____

_____

_____

_____

_____

_____

_____

_____

_____

_____

_____

_____

Many leadership problems are
driven by low self-awareness.

Bill Hybels

LEARN & LIVE – A-GAME

Now that you have completed today's contract and have had it scored, take a moment before you go to bed and answer the following questions:

What was I most proud of?

_____

_____

_____

_____

What was I least proud of?

_____

_____

_____

_____

What did I learn about myself?

_____

_____

_____

_____

What will I do differently in the future?

_____

_____

_____

_____

LIMITLESS

You can't wait for
what you want to
motivate you, so
everything must.

LIMITLESS

I, _____, hereby enter into this contract with myself, the Uncommon Competitor, and commit to learning TODAY'S FOCUS and completing all of the outlined RESPONSIBILITIES for the day.

_____   ____ /____ / 20____
Competitor (Signature)   Date

I. <u>TODAY'S FOCUS</u>

Reasons come first; answers come second. Uncommon Competitors are limitless because they have many reasons why to be motivated. You must take your whys very seriously so that you stay driven!

II. <u>RESPONSIBILITIES</u>

(1) Write down as many things as possible that can motivate you. Be sure to list reasons why to be motivated for the most challenging situations you can think of. Share your list with one person.

(2) Select a witness and teach them what you learned. Have them evaluate your teaching, give you a score and sign.

COMPETITOR TEACHING EVALUATION	
1 = Average 2 = Above Average 3 = Superior	
Clarity: Did they know the content and teach it clearly?	
Creativity: Did they teach in a unique way?	
Conviction: Did they teach with passion and confidence?	
Total Score	/9

IN WITNESS WHEREOF, I, _____, confirm that the Uncommon Competitor has completed the contract and I have honestly evaluated their teaching.

_____   ____ /____ / 20____
Witness (Signature)   Date

NOTES – LIMITLESS

Make hard work your motivation, not performance.

Anonymous

LEARN & LIVE – LIMITLESS

Now that you have completed today's contract and have had it scored, take a moment before you go to bed and answer the following questions:

What was I most proud of?

_____

_____

_____

_____

What was I least proud of?

_____

_____

_____

_____

What did I learn about myself?

_____

_____

_____

_____

What will I do differently in the future?

_____

_____

_____

_____

IF YOU ONLY KNEW

Honesty won't get
you a lot of friends;
it will get you the
right ones.

IF YOU ONLY KNEW

I, _____, hereby enter into this
contract with myself, the Uncommon Competitor, and commit to
learning TODAY'S FOCUS and completing all of the outlined
RESPONSIBILITIES for the day.

_____   ____ / ____ / 20____
Competitor (Signature)   Date

I. TODAY'S FOCUS

**There isn't anyone you couldn't love once you've learned
their story.** Uncommon Competitors are always sharing
personal information with others. You must communicate
with transparency so that others can trust you.

II. RESPONSIBILITIES

(1) Write down (one-page maximum) your most powerful past
accomplishments, hardships, experiences or anything else
of importance. Share your one-page with someone.

(2) Select a witness and teach them what you learned. Have
them evaluate your teaching, give you a score and sign.

COMPETITOR TEACHING EVALUATION	
1 = Average 2 = Above Average 3 = Superior	
Clarity: Did they know the content and teach it clearly?	
Creativity: Did they teach in a unique way?	
Conviction: Did they teach with passion and confidence?	
Total Score	/9

IN WITNESS WHEREOF, I, _____,
confirm that the Uncommon Competitor has completed the
contract and I have honestly evaluated their teaching.

_____   ____ / ____ / 20____
Witness (Signature)   Date

NOTES – IF YOU ONLY KNEW

Trust, honesty, humility, transparency and accountability
are the building blocks of a positive reputation.
Trust is the foundation of any relationship.

Mike Paul

LEARN & LIVE – IF YOU ONLY KNEW

Now that you have completed today's contract and have had it scored, take a moment before you go to bed and answer the following questions:

What was I most proud of?

_____

_____

_____

_____

What was I least proud of?

_____

_____

_____

_____

What did I learn about myself?

_____

_____

_____

_____

What will I do differently in the future?

_____

_____

_____

_____

SURVIVAL OF
THE WISEST

Ask a bad question
and be a fool for five
minutes, or never ask
a question and remain
a fool forever.

SURVIVAL OF THE WISEST

I, _____, hereby enter into this
contract with myself, the Uncommon Competitor, and commit to
learning TODAY'S FOCUS and completing all of the outlined
RESPONSIBILITIES for the day.

_____   ____ /____ / 20____
Competitor (Signature)   Date

I. TODAY'S FOCUS

**To find out what lies ahead ask the people on the way
back.** Uncommon Competitors listen to their elders. You
must learn from experience so that mistakes aren't repeated!

II. RESPONSIBILITIES

(1) Ask one person that is older than you these questions and
write down their answers: "What lesson took you the
longest to learn? What do you know that others don't?
What strategy solved your biggest struggle?"

(2) Select a witness and teach them what you learned. Have
them evaluate your teaching, give you a score and sign.

COMPETITOR TEACHING EVALUATION	
1 = Average 2 = Above Average 3 = Superior	
Clarity: Did they know the content and teach it clearly?	
Creativity: Did they teach in a unique way?	
Conviction: Did they teach with passion and confidence?	
Total Score	/9

IN WITNESS WHEREOF, I, _____,
confirm that the Uncommon Competitor has completed the
contract and I have honestly evaluated their teaching.

_____   ____ /____ / 20____
Witness (Signature)   Date

NOTES - SURVIVAL OF THE WISEST

NOTES – SURVIVAL OF THE WISEST

A wise man can learn more from a foolish question
than a fool can learn from a wise answer.

Bruce Lee

LEARN & LIVE – SURVIVAL OF THE WISEST

Now that you have completed today's contract and have had it scored, take a moment before you go to bed and answer the following questions:

What was I most proud of?

_____

_____

_____

_____

What was I least proud of?

_____

_____

_____

_____

What did I learn about myself?

_____

_____

_____

_____

What will I do differently in the future?

_____

_____

_____

_____

WORST-CASE SCENARIO

Under pressure, you'll never rise to the occasion. Instead, you'll rise, or fall based on the level of your training.

WORST-CASE SCENARIO

I, _____, hereby enter into this contract with myself, the Uncommon Competitor, and commit to learning TODAY'S FOCUS and completing all of the outlined RESPONSIBILITIES for the day.

_____   ____ / ____ / 20____
Competitor (Signature)   Date

I. <u>TODAY'S FOCUS</u>

To be your best you must always be training for the worst. Uncommon Competitors prepare for worst-case scenarios. You must discuss the most difficult situations so that you can better handle them when they happen!

II. <u>RESPONSIBILITIES</u>

(1) Discuss worst-case scenarios with someone (you're broke, a family member died, you're ill, etc.). After one is shared, respond positively by saying: "Good! Now I _____."

(2) Select a witness and teach them what you learned. Have them evaluate your teaching, give you a score and sign.

COMPETITOR TEACHING EVALUATION	
1 = Average 2 = Above Average 3 = Superior	
Clarity: Did they know the content and teach it clearly?	
Creativity: Did they teach in a unique way?	
Conviction: Did they teach with passion and confidence?	
Total Score	/9

IN WITNESS WHEREOF, I, _____, confirm that the Uncommon Competitor has completed the contract and I have honestly evaluated their teaching.

_____   ____ / ____ / 20____
Witness (Signature)   Date

NOTES - WORST-CASE SCENARIO

NOTES – WORST-CASE SCENARIO

_____

_____

_____

_____

_____

_____

_____

_____

_____

_____

_____

_____

_____

_____

_____

_____

_____

_____

_____

_____

_____

Practice isn't really practice unless the pressure is right.

Scott Savor

LEARN & LIVE – WORST-CASE SCENARIO

Now that you have completed today's contract and have had it scored, take a moment before you go to bed and answer the following questions:

What was I most proud of?

_____

_____

_____

_____

What was I least proud of?

_____

_____

_____

_____

What did I learn about myself?

_____

_____

_____

_____

What will I do differently in the future?

_____

_____

_____

_____

GOT YOUR
BACK

You can't help
another person
permanently by doing
for them what they
could and should do
for themselves.

GOT YOUR BACK

I, _____, hereby enter into this contract with myself, the Uncommon Competitor, and commit to learning TODAY'S FOCUS and completing all of the outlined RESPONSIBILITIES for the day.

_____   ____ / ____ / 20____
Competitor (Signature)   Date

I. <u>TODAY'S FOCUS</u>

Curiosity separates the truly alive from the ones merely going through the motions. Uncommon Competitors get others backs by checking-in consistently. You must remain passionately curious so that you can to help almost anyone!

II. <u>RESPONSIBILITIES</u>

(1) Ask one person the following questions and write down their answers: "What are your personal and professional goals? Are you reaching them? How can I help?"

(2) Select a witness and teach them what you learned. Have them evaluate your teaching, give you a score and sign.

COMPETITOR TEACHING EVALUATION	
1 = Average 2 = Above Average 3 = Superior	
Clarity: Did they know the content and teach it clearly?	
Creativity: Did they teach in a unique way?	
Conviction: Did they teach with passion and confidence?	
Total Score	/9

IN WITNESS WHEREOF, I, _____, confirm that the Uncommon Competitor has completed the contract and I have honestly evaluated their teaching.

_____   ____ / ____ / 20____
Witness (Signature)   Date

NOTES – GOT YOUR BACK

NOTES – GOT YOUR BACK

I cannot teach anybody anything.
I can only make them think.

Socrates

LEARN & LIVE – GOT YOUR BACK

Now that you have completed today's contract and have had it scored, take a moment before you go to bed and answer the following questions:

What was I most proud of?

_____

_____

_____

_____

What was I least proud of?

_____

_____

_____

_____

What did I learn about myself?

_____

_____

_____

_____

What will I do differently in the future?

_____

_____

_____

_____

GET YOUR
MIND RIGHT

If you are depressed,
you are living in
the past.

If you are anxious,
you are living in
the future.

If you are at peace,
you are living in
the present.

GET YOUR MIND RIGHT

I, _____, hereby enter into this
contract with myself, the Uncommon Competitor, and commit to
learning TODAY'S FOCUS and completing all of the outlined
RESPONSIBILITIES for the day.

_____   ____ / ____ / 20____
Competitor (Signature)   Date

I. TODAY'S FOCUS

Quit trying to calm the storm, calm yourself. Uncommon
Competitors get their mind right by creating calmness. You
must have options to reset and relax so that you can take
control!

II. RESPONSIBILITIES

(1) Sit down and listen carefully to one or more of the
following peaceful songs: "Weightless" by Marconi Union,
"Giving You the Best That I've Got" by Anita Baker or
"Canzonetta Sull'aria" by Mozart.

(2) Select a witness and teach them what you learned. Have
them evaluate your teaching, give you a score and sign.

COMPETITOR TEACHING EVALUATION	
1 = Average 2 = Above Average 3 = Superior	
Clarity: Did they know the content and teach it clearly?	
Creativity: Did they teach in a unique way?	
Conviction: Did they teach with passion and confidence?	
Total Score	/9

IN WITNESS WHEREOF, I, _____,
confirm that the Uncommon Competitor has completed the
contract and I have honestly evaluated their teaching.

_____   ____ / ____ / 20____
Witness (Signature)   Date

NOTES – GET YOUR MIND RIGHT

NOTES – GET YOUR MIND RIGHT

_____

_____

_____

_____

_____

_____

_____

_____

_____

_____

_____

_____

_____

_____

_____

_____

_____

_____

_____

_____

_____

_____

The quieter you become, the more you can hear.

Ram Dass

LEARN & LIVE – GET YOUR MIND RIGHT

Now that you have completed today's contract and have had it
scored, take a moment before you go to bed and answer the
following questions:

What was I most proud of?

_____

_____

_____

_____

What was I least proud of?

_____

_____

_____

_____

What did I learn about myself?

_____

_____

_____

_____

What will I do differently in the future?

_____

_____

_____

_____

PERFORMANCE
PLAYLIST

No matter what the adversity, music can help you through it.

PERFORMANCE PLAYLIST

I, _____, hereby enter into this
contract with myself, the Uncommon Competitor, and commit to
learning TODAY'S FOCUS and completing all of the outlined
RESPONSIBILITIES for the day.

_____   ____ / ____ / 20____
Competitor (Signature)   Date

I. TODAY'S FOCUS

Music is the medicine of the mind. Uncommon
Competitors use specific music to improve their emotional
performance. You must assess and adjust your feelings so that
you can assist others with theirs!

II. RESPONSIBILITIES

(1) Create slow, moderate and fast playlists. Tired? Play the
fast list. Nervous? Play the slow list. Confident? Play the
moderate list. The goal is to stay in the moderate zone.

(2) Select a witness and teach them what you learned. Have
them evaluate your teaching, give you a score and sign.

COMPETITOR TEACHING EVALUATION	
1 = Average 2 = Above Average 3 = Superior	
Clarity: Did they know the content and teach it clearly?	
Creativity: Did they teach in a unique way?	
Conviction: Did they teach with passion and confidence?	
Total Score	**/9**

IN WITNESS WHEREOF, I, _____,
confirm that the Uncommon Competitor has completed the
contract and I have honestly evaluated their teaching.

_____   ____ / ____ / 20____
Witness (Signature)   Date

NOTES – PERFORMANCE PLAYLIST

NOTES – PERFORMANCE PLAYLIST

_____

_____

_____

_____

_____

_____

_____

_____

_____

_____

_____

_____

_____

_____

_____

_____

_____

_____

Those who dance the dance of life appear insane
to those who can't hear the music.

Anonymous

LEARN & LIVE – PERFORMANCE PLAYLIST

Now that you have completed today's contract and have had it scored, take a moment before you go to bed and answer the following questions:

What was I most proud of?

_____

_____

_____

_____

What was I least proud of?

_____

_____

_____

_____

What did I learn about myself?

_____

_____

_____

_____

What will I do differently in the future?

_____

_____

_____

_____

PROUD
PURCHASE

When health is
absent, wisdom
cannot reveal itself,
abilities cannot
manifest, strength
cannot fight, and
intelligence cannot
be applied.

PROUD PURCHASE

I, _____, hereby enter into this
contract with myself, the Uncommon Competitor, and commit to
learning TODAY'S FOCUS and completing all of the outlined
RESPONSIBILITIES for the day.

_____   ____ / ____ / 20____
Competitor (Signature)   Date

I. TODAY'S FOCUS

**Health isn't just what you're eating; it's what you're
thinking and saying.** Uncommon Competitors purchase
things they're proud of to improve their health. You must
invest in things that will enhance you mentally, physically,
emotionally and spiritually so that you can truly enjoy life!

II. RESPONSIBILITIES

(1) Ask one person what their top three purchases they're
proud of are and write them down. Create your own top
three list (to be purchased items) and then buy one.

(2) Select a witness and teach them what you learned. Have
them evaluate your teaching, give you a score and sign.

COMPETITOR TEACHING EVALUATION	
1 = Average 2 = Above Average 3 = Superior	
Clarity: Did they know the content and teach it clearly?	
Creativity: Did they teach in a unique way?	
Conviction: Did they teach with passion and confidence?	
Total Score	/9

IN WITNESS WHEREOF, I, _____,
confirm that the Uncommon Competitor has completed the
contract and I have honestly evaluated their teaching.

_____   ____ / ____ / 20____
Witness (Signature)   Date

NOTES – PROUD PURCHASE

NOTES – PROUD PURCHASE

*When I get a little money, I buy books; and
if any is left I buy food and clothes.*

Desiderius Erasmus

LEARN & LIVE – PROUD PURCHASE

Now that you have completed today's contract and have had it scored, take a moment before you go to bed and answer the following questions:

What was I most proud of?

_____

_____

_____

_____

What was I least proud of?

_____

_____

_____

_____

What did I learn about myself?

_____

_____

_____

_____

What will I do differently in the future?

_____

_____

_____

_____

STRENGTH IN NUMBERS

If you want to
influence someone,
ask better questions.

STRENGTH IN NUMBERS

I, _____, hereby enter into this
contract with myself, the Uncommon Competitor, and commit to
learning TODAY'S FOCUS and completing all of the outlined
RESPONSIBILITIES for the day.

_____   ____ / ____ / 20____
Competitor (Signature)   Date

I. TODAY'S FOCUS

Two is better than one only when two behave as one.
Uncommon Competitors believe there is strength in numbers.
You must go out of your way to collaborate so that everyone
can be more useful!

II. RESPONSIBILITIES

(1) Teach one person a responsibility, skill or daily routine you
have. Write down their answers to the following: "What do
you think? Any questions? What can I do better?"

(2) Select a witness and teach them what you learned. Have
them evaluate your teaching, give you a score and sign.

COMPETITOR TEACHING EVALUATION	
1 = Average 2 = Above Average 3 = Superior	
Clarity: Did they know the content and teach it clearly?	
Creativity: Did they teach in a unique way?	
Conviction: Did they teach with passion and confidence?	
Total Score	/9

IN WITNESS WHEREOF, I, _____,
confirm that the Uncommon Competitor has completed the
contract and I have honestly evaluated their teaching.

_____   ____ / ____ / 20____
Witness (Signature)   Date

137

NOTES – STRENGTH IN NUMBERS

NOTES – STRENGTH IN NUMBERS

When we argue for our limitations, we get to keep them.

Evelyn Waugh

LEARN & LIVE – STRENGTH IN NUMBERS

Now that you have completed today's contract and have had it scored, take a moment before you go to bed and answer the following questions:

What was I most proud of?

_____

_____

_____

_____

What was I least proud of?

_____

_____

_____

_____

What did I learn about myself?

_____

_____

_____

_____

What will I do differently in the future?

_____

_____

_____

_____

GIVE UP
TO GO UP

Happiness is not
found in seeking
more, but in
developing the
capacity to enjoy less.

GIVE UP TO GO UP

I, _____, hereby enter into this
contract with myself, the Uncommon Competitor, and commit to
learning TODAY'S FOCUS and completing all of the outlined
RESPONSIBILITIES for the day.

_____   ____ / ____ / 20___
Competitor (Signature)   Date

I. TODAY'S FOCUS

Those who live simply sleep soundly. Uncommon
Competitors "give up" materialistic items in order "to go up"
and improve their lifestyle. You must delete the number of
things you own so that you can dedicate more time to people!

II. RESPONSIBILITIES

(1) Examine your things (electronics, toys, computer files,
furniture, clothing, etc.). For every five things, give up one
thing. Celebrate everything you eliminate.

(2) Select a witness and teach them what you learned. Have
them evaluate your teaching, give you a score and sign.

COMPETITOR TEACHING EVALUATION	
1 = Average 2 = Above Average 3 = Superior	
Clarity: Did they know the content and teach it clearly?	
Creativity: Did they teach in a unique way?	
Conviction: Did they teach with passion and confidence?	
Total Score	/9

IN WITNESS WHEREOF, I, _____,
confirm that the Uncommon Competitor has completed the
contract and I have honestly evaluated their teaching.

_____   ____ / ____ / 20___
Witness (Signature)   Date

NOTES – GIVE UP TO GO UP

To attain knowledge, add things every day.
To attain wisdom, remove things every day.

Lao Tzu

LEARN & LIVE – GIVE UP TO GO UP

Now that you have completed today's contract and have had it scored, take a moment before you go to bed and answer the following questions:

What was I most proud of?

_____

_____

_____

_____

What was I least proud of?

_____

_____

_____

_____

What did I learn about myself?

_____

_____

_____

_____

What will I do differently in the future?

_____

_____

_____

_____

CELL PHONE ROULETTE

Become interested in a person, and the more interesting they become. Everything you see on the inside of them you can now see on the outside.

CELL PHONE ROULETTE

I, _____, hereby enter into this contract with myself, the Uncommon Competitor, and commit to learning TODAY'S FOCUS and completing all of the outlined RESPONSIBILITIES for the day.

_____   ____ / ____ / 20____
Competitor (Signature)   Date

I. <u>TODAY'S FOCUS</u>

No one is an actual friend until they defend you in your absence. Uncommon Competitors defend the contacts in their phones. You must open your inner circle to others so that they can open theirs to you.

II. <u>RESPONSIBILITIES</u>

(1) Open your phone contacts list with someone. Take turns swiping a list, sharing a name and why they are important to you (30 seconds or less).

(2) Select a witness and teach them what you learned. Have them evaluate your teaching, give you a score and sign.

COMPETITOR TEACHING EVALUATION	
1 = Average 2 = Above Average 3 = Superior	
Clarity: Did they know the content and teach it clearly?	
Creativity: Did they teach in a unique way?	
Conviction: Did they teach with passion and confidence?	
Total Score	/9

IN WITNESS WHEREOF, I, _____, confirm that the Uncommon Competitor has completed the contract and I have honestly evaluated their teaching.

_____   ____ / ____ / 20____
Witness (Signature)   Date

NOTES – CELL PHONE ROULETTE

NOTES – CELL PHONE ROULETTE

_____

_____

_____

_____

_____

_____

_____

_____

_____

_____

_____

_____

_____

_____

_____

_____

_____

_____

_____

_____

_____

_____

*Hang out with the ones who heard you
when you never said a word.*

Unknown

LEARN & LIVE – CELL PHONE ROULETTE

Now that you have completed today's contract and have had it scored, take a moment before you go to bed and answer the following questions:

What was I most proud of?

_____

_____

_____

_____

What was I least proud of?

_____

_____

_____

_____

What did I learn about myself?

_____

_____

_____

_____

What will I do differently in the future?

_____

_____

_____

_____

REFUEL

No rest is worth
anything except the
rest that is earned.

REFUEL

I, _____, hereby enter into this contract with myself, the Uncommon Competitor, and commit to learning TODAY'S FOCUS and completing all of the outlined RESPONSIBILITIES for the day.

_____   ____ /____ / 20____
Competitor (Signature)   Date

I. <u>TODAY'S FOCUS</u>

Treat rest as a necessity, not an objective, only rest long enough to gather strength. Uncommon Competitors know the difference between resting and refueling. You must refuel with no regrets so that you are ready for anything at any time!

II. <u>RESPONSIBILITIES</u>

(1) Choose your nap time: 20 minutes (energy boost), 60 minutes (short-term memory increase) or 90 minutes (creativity improves). Set your alarm and refuel.

(2) Select a witness and teach them what you learned. Have them evaluate your teaching, give you a score and sign.

COMPETITOR TEACHING EVALUATION	
1 = Average 2 = Above Average 3 = Superior	
Clarity: Did they know the content and teach it clearly?	
Creativity: Did they teach in a unique way?	
Conviction: Did they teach with passion and confidence?	
Total Score	/9

IN WITNESS WHEREOF, I, _____, confirm that the Uncommon Competitor has completed the contract and I have honestly evaluated their teaching.

_____   ____ /____ / 20____
Witness (Signature)   Date

NOTES – REFUEL

NOTES – REFUEL

If you love someone, let them nap.

Unknown

LEARN & LIVE – REFUEL

Now that you have completed today's contract and have had it scored, take a moment before you go to bed and answer the following questions:

What was I most proud of?

_____

_____

_____

_____

What was I least proud of?

_____

_____

_____

_____

What did I learn about myself?

_____

_____

_____

_____

What will I do differently in the future?

_____

_____

_____

_____

BUILT FOR
THE GRIND

When you discover
you can walk on
water that's when you
take the boat.

BUILT FOR THE GRIND

I, _____, hereby enter into this contract with myself, the Uncommon Competitor, and commit to learning TODAY'S FOCUS and completing all of the outlined RESPONSIBILITIES for the day.

_____   ____ / ____ / 20____
Competitor (Signature)   Date

I. TODAY'S FOCUS

The only reward for a job well done is harder work.
Uncommon Competitors are "built for the grind" because they are always testing their toughness. You must ask others to challenge you even more so that your skills keep improving!

II. RESPONSIBILITIES

(1) Test your toughness on a task. Ask someone: "Can you make _____ tougher?" Write down their reaction and how they increased the difficulty.

(2) Select a witness and teach them what you learned. Have them evaluate your teaching, give you a score and sign.

COMPETITOR TEACHING EVALUATION	
1 = Average　2 = Above Average　3 = Superior	
Clarity: Did they know the content and teach it clearly?	
Creativity: Did they teach in a unique way?	
Conviction: Did they teach with passion and confidence?	
Total Score	/9

IN WITNESS WHEREOF, I, _____,
confirm that the Uncommon Competitor has completed the contract and I have honestly evaluated their teaching.

_____   ____ / ____ / 20____
Witness (Signature)   Date

NOTES – BUILT FOR THE GRIND

NOTES – BUILT FOR THE GRIND

Adversity makes men, and prosperity makes monsters.

Victor Hugo

LEARN & LIVE – BUILT FOR THE GRIND

Now that you have completed today's contract and have had it scored, take a moment before you go to bed and answer the following questions:

What was I most proud of?

_____

_____

_____

_____

What was I least proud of?

_____

_____

_____

_____

What did I learn about myself?

_____

_____

_____

_____

What will I do differently in the future?

_____

_____

_____

_____

DEDICATION DAY

Obsessed is a
word the lazy use
to describe the
dedicated.

DEDICATION DAY

I, _____, hereby enter into this
contract with myself, the Uncommon Competitor, and commit to
learning TODAY'S FOCUS and completing all of the outlined
RESPONSIBILITIES for the day.

_____   ___ / ___ / 20___
Competitor (Signature)   Date

I. <u>TODAY'S FOCUS</u>

Teamwork divides the task and multiplies the success.
Uncommon Competitors dedicate days to others to maximize
everyone's effectiveness. You must compete for someone so
that your inspiration and influence increases!

II. <u>RESPONSIBILITIES</u>

(1) Write down five people who would be most influenced if
you accomplished your goals today. Choose one person,
share your goals and then work hard for them.

(2) Select a witness and teach them what you learned. Have
them evaluate your teaching, give you a score and sign.

COMPETITOR TEACHING EVALUATION	
1 = Average 2 = Above Average 3 = Superior	
Clarity: Did they know the content and teach it clearly?	
Creativity: Did they teach in a unique way?	
Conviction: Did they teach with passion and confidence?	
Total Score	/9

IN WITNESS WHEREOF, I, _____,
confirm that the Uncommon Competitor has completed the
contract and I have honestly evaluated their teaching.

_____   ___ / ___ / 20___
Witness (Signature)   Date

NOTES – DEDICATION DAY

NOTES – DEDICATION DAY

_____

_____

_____

_____

_____

_____

_____

_____

_____

_____

_____

_____

_____

_____

_____

_____

_____

_____

_____

_____

_____

_____

_____

Every crisis faced together makes the circle stronger.

Harriet Morgan

LEARN & LIVE – DEDICATION DAY

Now that you have completed today's contract and have had it scored, take a moment before you go to bed and answer the following questions:

What was I most proud of?

_____

_____

_____

_____

What was I least proud of?

_____

_____

_____

_____

What did I learn about myself?

_____

_____

_____

_____

What will I do differently in the future?

_____

_____

_____

_____

PERSONAL
THANK YOU

Be thankful for the
people in your life
who would drive five
hours just to see
you for one.

PERSONAL THANK YOU

I, _____, hereby enter into this
contract with myself, the Uncommon Competitor, and commit to
learning TODAY'S FOCUS and completing all of the outlined
RESPONSIBILITIES for the day.

_____   ____ / ____ / 20____
Competitor (Signature)   Date

I. TODAY'S FOCUS

**Imagine if you woke up tomorrow with only the things
you were thankful for today.** Uncommon Competitors
consistently thank those who are valuable to them. You must
express precisely why you are grateful for others so that the
beneficial behavior is repeated!

II. RESPONSIBILITIES

(1) Create a "personal thank you" video message for someone
(one minute or less). Be sincere and specific.

(2) Select a witness and teach them what you learned. Have
them evaluate your teaching, give you a score and sign.

COMPETITOR TEACHING EVALUATION	
1 = Average 2 = Above Average 3 = Superior	
Clarity: Did they know the content and teach it clearly?	
Creativity: Did they teach in a unique way?	
Conviction: Did they teach with passion and confidence?	
Total Score	/9

IN WITNESS WHEREOF, I, _____,
confirm that the Uncommon Competitor has completed the
contract and I have honestly evaluated their teaching.

_____   ____ / ____ / 20____
Witness (Signature)   Date

NOTES – PERSONAL THANK YOU

NOTES – PERSONAL THANK YOU

The greatest weakness of most humans is their hesitancy to tell others how much they love them while they're alive.

Optimus Prime

LEARN & LIVE – PERSONAL THANK YOU

Now that you have completed today's contract and have had it scored, take a moment before you go to bed and answer the following questions:

What was I most proud of?

_____

_____

_____

_____

What was I least proud of?

_____

_____

_____

_____

What did I learn about myself?

_____

_____

_____

_____

What will I do differently in the future?

_____

_____

_____

_____

CHANGE THE WORLD LIST

Stop focusing on what you can accomplish, instead focus on how much you can absolutely love what you're doing.

CHANGE THE WORLD LIST

I, _____, hereby enter into this
contract with myself, the Uncommon Competitor, and commit to
learning TODAY'S FOCUS and completing all of the outlined
RESPONSIBILITIES for the day.

_____   ____ / ____ / 20____
Competitor (Signature)   Date

I. TODAY'S FOCUS

**Brag about how busy you are, and you'll never be able to
brag about how balanced you are.** Uncommon
Competitors have a strategic "change the world list." You
must focus on fewer things so that you don't destroy yourself!

II. RESPONSIBILITIES

(1) Write down 20 goals. Execute your top five based on the
following: Does it develop relationships and skills? Does it
make other goals easier or irrelevant? Does it excite me?

(2) Select a witness and teach them what you learned. Have
them evaluate your teaching, give you a score and sign.

COMPETITOR TEACHING EVALUATION	
1 = Average 2 = Above Average 3 = Superior	
Clarity: Did they know the content and teach it clearly?	
Creativity: Did they teach in a unique way?	
Conviction: Did they teach with passion and confidence?	
Total Score	/9

IN WITNESS WHEREOF, I, _____,
confirm that the Uncommon Competitor has completed the
contract and I have honestly evaluated their teaching.

_____   ____ / ____ / 20____
Witness (Signature)   Date

179

NOTES – CHANGE THE WORLD LIST

NOTES – CHANGE THE WORLD LIST

_____
_____
_____
_____
_____
_____
_____
_____
_____
_____
_____
_____
_____
_____
_____
_____
_____
_____
_____
_____

What you do today can improve all your tomorrows.

Ralph Marston

LEARN & LIVE – CHANGE THE WORLD LIST

Now that you have completed today's contract and have had it scored, take a moment before you go to bed and answer the following questions:

What was I most proud of?

_____

_____

_____

_____

What was I least proud of?

_____

_____

_____

_____

What did I learn about myself?

_____

_____

_____

_____

What will I do differently in the future?

_____

_____

_____

_____

LI'L MO

A good leader sustains momentum; a great leader increases it.

LI'L MO

I, _____, hereby enter into this
contract with myself, the Uncommon Competitor, and commit to
learning TODAY'S FOCUS and completing all of the outlined
RESPONSIBILITIES for the day.

_____   ____ /____ / 20___
Competitor (Signature)   Date

I. <u>TODAY'S FOCUS</u>

Excitement must lead to action or momentum is lost.
Uncommon Competitors make a "little momentum" by
celebrating little things in a big way. You must reward the
process so that momentum can help solve your problems!

II. <u>RESPONSIBILITIES</u>

(1) Identify and write down how three people demonstrated
exceptional attitude, effort or focus today. Celebrate their
behavior in an uncommon way (high five, dance, etc.).

(2) Select a witness and teach them what you learned. Have
them evaluate your teaching, give you a score and sign.

COMPETITOR TEACHING EVALUATION	
1 = Average 2 = Above Average 3 = Superior	
Clarity: Did they know the content and teach it clearly?	
Creativity: Did they teach in a unique way?	
Conviction: Did they teach with passion and confidence?	
Total Score	/9

IN WITNESS WHEREOF, I, _____,
confirm that the Uncommon Competitor has completed the
contract and I have honestly evaluated their teaching.

_____   ____ /____ / 20___
Witness (Signature)   Date

185

NOTES – LI'L MO

NOTES – LI'L MO

You must make the little things feel like big things.

Anonymous

LEARN & LIVE – LI'L MO

Now that you have completed today's contract and have had it scored, take a moment before you go to bed and answer the following questions:

What was I most proud of?

_____

_____

_____

_____

What was I least proud of?

_____

_____

_____

_____

What did I learn about myself?

_____

_____

_____

_____

What will I do differently in the future?

_____

_____

_____

_____

F.O.T.D.

Don't fear failure.
Fear being in the
exact same place next
year as you are today.

F.O.T.D

I, _____, hereby enter into this contract with myself, the Uncommon Competitor, and commit to learning TODAY'S FOCUS and completing all of the outlined RESPONSIBILITIES for the day.

_____   ____ / ____ / 20____
Competitor (Signature)   Date

I. <u>TODAY'S FOCUS</u>

Fear destroys more dreams than failure ever will.
Uncommon Competitors aren't afraid to discuss their "Failure Of The Day" with anyone. You must create a mistake driven culture so that you compete confidently and not fear failure!

II. <u>RESPONSIBILITIES</u>

(1) Select one person and write down the answers to these: "What was your worst failure ever? What was the worst failure you've witnessed? What was your F.O.T.D.?"

(2) Select a witness and teach them what you learned. Have them evaluate your teaching, give you a score and sign.

COMPETITOR TEACHING EVALUATION	
1 = Average 2 = Above Average 3 = Superior	
Clarity: Did they know the content and teach it clearly?	
Creativity: Did they teach in a unique way?	
Conviction: Did they teach with passion and confidence?	
Total Score	/9

IN WITNESS WHEREOF, I, _____, confirm that the Uncommon Competitor has completed the contract and I have honestly evaluated their teaching.

_____   ____ / ____ / 20____
Witness (Signature)   Date

NOTES – F.O.T.D.

NOTES – F.O.T.D.

_____

_____

_____

_____

_____

_____

_____

_____

_____

_____

_____

_____

_____

_____

_____

_____

_____

_____

_____

_____

_____

Your failures won't hurt you until you start
blaming them on others.

Zig Ziglar

LEARN & LIVE – F.O.T.D.

Now that you have completed today's contract and have had it scored, take a moment before you go to bed and answer the following questions:

What was I most proud of?

_____

_____

_____

_____

What was I least proud of?

_____

_____

_____

_____

What did I learn about myself?

_____

_____

_____

_____

What will I do differently in the future?

_____

_____

_____

_____

SCORING YOUR PERFORMANCE

HOW WELL DID YOU DO?

I hope that what you needed arrived for you the last 30 days. Whether you completed one or all the 30 contracts, achieved "average" or "superior" scores on your teaching evaluations, everything you did mattered because you created momentum and made a choice to be uncommon. I'm proud of you.

Scoring Your Performance		
Competitor Level	**Total Completed**	**Teaching Score**
Common	0 – 7 contracts	0 – 65
Slightly Uncommon	8 – 15 contracts	66 – 130
Almost Uncommon	16 – 24 contracts	131 – 202
Uncommon	25 – 30 contracts	203+

Was your uncommon behavior acknowledged or rewarded during the 30-day process? If not, you must immediately step your game up and get around more value-driven people who make rewarding the process a priority. In life, we most often have the privilege to choose what we do next.

Now the question that lies ahead is this: What comes next? There was a time when it was believed that it took 21 days to develop a new habit (or break an old one), but in reality, this is only true for simple things. New research shows that for true change to occur, especially in terms of more complex habits, the average time is closer to 66 days.

While there were a wide variety of strategies within this book, the core habit to be developed was discipline and starting each day with something that kept your focus on your vision and core values. This is what would be considered a complex habit. Take a moment and ask yourself these questions:

- As you were going through the daily contracts, did you have to remind yourself or force yourself to get it done, for all 30 days? Were there any that you were not able to complete?

- Without the physical contracts as a reminder, do you feel you have 100% become a highly disciplined and hyper-focused person in the pursuit of your purpose?

If you are like most people, the answers will be "Yes" and "No" but don't feel bad, because according to research, you are only halfway there. It's time to commit yourself to another 30 days if you are truly serious about separating yourself from the competition. For those of you who had great success, and found the process of tremendous value, I also recommend sticking with the habit! That was the goal in the first place, right?

Now, there are several ways you can approach this:

- **Option 1**: Strategically, the most effective option is to repeat the process using the same 30 contracts, perhaps changing the order around this time. Using this option gives you both the exposure to multiple strategies, avoiding boredom, and allows you to focus on the ones that gave you difficulty without becoming overwhelmed. This time go a bit further with the responsibility of the day. For example, choose a different person, re-examine a previous list, modify or elaborate on it, or for the ones you struggled with, repeat as is.

- **Option 2:** Choose to repeat the contracts that gave you more difficulty on more than one day, ensuring that in the end, you have 30 days of contracts. How you do this is a matter of personal style. Some of you will want to commit to the same focus a few days in a row, others will want to alternate them.

- **Option 3:** For those of you who are confident in their own self-discipline, create your own daily habit, and implement it every day. I recommend getting a journal of some type to record your progress and hold yourself accountable to daily actions.

It is my recommendation that you purchase a new book for repeating the process because there is power in having the tangible book in your hand. In the end, you will have an organized, recorded history of your journey.

For those of you who found this process of no value or easier than you expected, I would like to ask that you please send me any feedback you have so that I can improve the book in the future.

Finally, I am very thankful and honored that you purchased my book and chose to compete uncommonly. Please contact me if there is anything I can do to help you in the future. Best of luck as you continue to separate yourself from the competition!

ABOUT THE
AUTHOR

WHO IS SCOTT SAVOR?

Scott Savor is the Founder and CEO of Uncommon Competitor, LLC. He is an author, professional speaker and coach for teams, companies, and individuals on leadership, motivation and mental training.

Scott received a bachelor's degree in Physical Education in Exercise Science with a minor in Coaching from Minnesota State University-Moorhead and a master's degree in Kinesiology with a concentration in Sports Psychology and Motor Learning from the University of Tennessee.

His purpose is to inspire improvement and he believes that living differently is the difference. Your purchases, leisure time, technology use and conversations all make up your lifestyle. Scott believes that to compete at the highest level professionally you must first focus on how you live personally.

NOTABLE ACCOMPLISHMENTS:

- Invested over 15,000 hours on personal and professional development on the subjects of motivation, philosophy, wealth, performance, psychology, leadership and business.
- Worked with NBA, WNBA, collegiate, and high school championship coaches, players, and teams.
- Coached/Consulted executive leaders of small businesses and multi-million-dollar companies.
- Featured in *Club Business for Entrepreneurs: Courting the Pros.*
- Featured in *Minnesota State University Alumnews: Weight Vision Quest.*

- Mission Leadership Award Nominee, University of Detroit Mercy.
- Co-Authored the book: *The Female Athlete: Reach for Victory.*

TOPICS PRESENTED:

- One-Day Contracts
- Why Winners Win
- Living Like a Leader
- Creating an Uncommon Culture
- Controlling the Controllables: Attitude, Effort, and Focus
- Culture Shock: What the Best Companies Aren't Doing
- Uncommon Leadership/Motivational/Mental Training Strategies and Solutions

CONTACT SCOTT:

If you enjoyed this book, have any questions or want to provide feedback for improvement, Scott would love to hear from you!

Interested in personal coaching with Scott? Contact him for information about his FREE 5-day coaching offer. Space is limited.

Need a different voice to inspire, engage and educate your team or company? Scott is available for group coaching and public speaking engagements.

SCOTT SAVOR
Founder/CEO
Uncommon Competitor LLC
248-217-9725
@ScottSavor
ScottSavor@gmail.com
www.ScottSavor.com